When We Rise

Chapter Questions Included

*To Patrice Whitted
From Patricia
Daboh 3/30/19*

Patricia Daboh

Copright © 2018 Patricia Daboh

All rights reserved.

ISBN-13: 978-1719503655

DEDICATION

Dedicated to all those who love the Lord Jesus and desire to prioritize him in their lives. May your thirst be quenched by God's holy presence!

CONTENTS

	Acknowledgments	i
	Foreword	1
1	When We Rise	6
2	A Made-Up Mind	25
3	Spiritual Deal Breakers	40
4	How Thirsty Are You?	51
5	Walking In the Valley With God	59
6	Exposed for Our Good	72
7	The Road of Recovery	84
8	Persevere Through It All	97
9	About the Author	108
10	Contact the Author	109

This book or parts thereof may not be reproduced in any form, stored in a retrieval system or transmitted in any form by any means—electronic, mechanical, photocopy, recording, or otherwise—without prior written permission of the author, except as provided by United States of America copyright law.

Unless otherwise noted, all Scripture quotations are from the King James Version of the Bible. King James Version is public domain.

Scripture quotations taken from the Amplified® Bible (AMP), Copyright © 2015 by The Lockman Foundation. Used by permission. www.Lockman.org.

Scripture quotations marked (ERV) are taken from the Holy Bible: Easy-to-Read Version, Copyright © 2006 by World Bible Translation Center, Inc., and used by permission.

Scripture quotations marked ESV are from the ESV® Bible (The Holy Bible, English Standard Version®), copyright © 2001 by Crossway, a publishing ministry of Good News Publishers. Used by permission.

Scripture quotations marked NIV are from the Holy Bible, New International Version. Copyright © 1973, 1978, 1984, 2010, 2011. International Bible Society. Used by permission.

Scripture quotations marked NKJV are from the New King James Version of the Bible. Copyright © 1979, 1980, 1982 by Thomas Nelson, Inc., publishers. Used by permission.

Scripture quotations marked NLT are from the Holy Bible, New Living Translation, copyright © 1996. Used by permission of Tyndale House Publishers, Inc., Wheaton, IL.

ACKNOWLEDGMENTS

To my family who loves me beyond words can describe and support my endeavors.

To my spiritual leaders who dedicate themselves to God, so you can impart an anointed word from heaven. Your right-on-time messages encourage and strengthen me.

To my brothers and sisters in Christ who embrace me, pray for me, and stand in the gap for me when I pass through fiery trials.

FOREWORD

There are moments in our lives that cause us to reflect on where we have come from, where we are now, and how much further we must go to achieve a feeling of accomplishment. While reflecting on these things, there are memories that cause us to celebrate our achievements from once defeated life moments. When I think about those times, it gives me strength to know that I somehow managed to have help from people and resources at just the right times.

While others lean on therapy, counselors and various forms of medications, there are others who lean on God and the testimony the Bible brings from others who witnessed struggle, hardship, infidelities, and temptations. Psalm 27 gives those who have faith in God the encouragement to know that "in the times of trouble, He shall hide us in the secrets of His tabernacle…"

In my life's journey, I would not have been able to survive or move on from the darkest places of my life if it had not been for my foundation in the Word of God. No matter what my life circumstances were, it was my relationship with God that helped continue my life in a more positive direction. However, there was a time that I felt that my relationship with God could not be repaired because of the decisions I chose to make that gave me negative consequences. Who should I blame? How do I begin to make sense of what I have done? With so many questions when you reach your darkest place in life, it is helpful to have a spiritual roadmap to help you maneuver through to recovery.

What happens to those who have nothing to reference? What happens to those who have no one to turn to when life turns to despair? What happens to those who have risked everything in pursuit of lustful gains only to lose everything and not recover anything?

Reading *When We Rise,* gives me a concrete roadmap and another foundation as a resource to turn to when I need help in kicking my life and spiritual path back into gear. We are not exempt from temptations and troubles no matter how good our life may appear to be seen on the outside. When we get into ourselves, through reflection, we realize that we are not perfect and have many imperfections. We need to have resources to help us make sense of it all.

Our reflections of those dark moments, those sinful life moments that helped us realize and acknowledge that we need help to start our journey of recovery are enlightening. How do we start our journey of recovery?

When We Rise gives us a roadmap to recovery and encouragement to know that though we may reach the lowest parts of our lives, we will rise to a better day. *When We Rise* gives us a foreshadow before we reach our darkest moments and describes how to obtain a better life in God. After reading *When We Rise*, I have hope that if my life gets off the path of how I am expected to live according to how the Word of God wants me to, I can rise again. We all can rise again! When we reach our darkest moments of life in sin, we must remember that eventually, we will rise to a better way of life. We will rise to a better living. We will rise to a stronger relationship with God. We will rise to endless possibilities towards success.

Patricia Daboh has tapped into the depths of her life to give us what we need to make our next step toward recovery possible, so we can envision and work towards rising to a new life in God. I thank God for another resource to lean on in times of trouble or in my darkest moment of life.

                                            Terence Jackson

1

WHEN WE RISE

Technology Versus Prayer

I found myself rising in the morning and reaching for my cell phone that I placed on the nightstand before going to sleep. I spent 5 or 10 minutes checking my nonprofit's Facebook page, my personal Facebook page, my emails, and scrolling through my other social media pages before it dawned on me that I had not even thanked God for allowing me to see another day. I felt irritated at myself for starting my day with technology—rather than with prayer and thanksgiving to God. I was determined never (ever) to let this happen again, but it happened again—more times than I would like to admit. Even before the smartphone emerged on the scene, I loved technology—having been a middle school and college computer teacher. My admiration and appreciation of technology and all its advancements is evident in the purchases I have made.

Technology is a force in our lives, and depending on your age, you may not know what it is like to not have a smartphone at your fingertips. The evolution of the cell phone is amazing, for it has far surpassed being used merely as a device to communicate. Along with this evolving technology, however, is an allure to always stay connected with it throughout our day. The struggle to prioritize God in our lives—from the moment our eyes open to see a new day until the time we close our eyes in sleep at night can be challenging for most of us. The battle to place God in the forefront of our lives is not being fought on a field with powerful weapons, but it's silently being fought with gadgets and activities that we enjoy—to the point that we spend hour-upon-hour consumed, entertained, and intrigued by them each day. Our focus is being shifted, and therefore, our priorities are changing.

Technology Versus Communication

I once saw a painting in which a grandmother was in the kitchen preparing a traditional Christmas dinner, and her grandchildren were gathered in the living room. No one was interacting with one another, for there were no conversations or laughter taking place. The grandchildren didn't seem curious about what the grandmother was cooking in the kitchen for Christmas dinner, and the grandmother seemed accustomed to not expecting much conversation from them. The low lighting in the living room, illuminated by a Christmas tree, cast a soft glow on the children's faces as they played with their technology devices (smartphones, tablets, laptops, etc.). The children's intense expressions revealed where their focus was. That painting accurately captured where technology influences have led us to. There is absolutely nothing wrong with having technology devices, but they should not be a substitution for quality moments God blesses us with to enjoy our loved ones. If we are less communicative or interactive with our family and friends whom we see, how are we communicating and interacting with God who we cannot see.

I have experienced someone not communicating with me as much as I wanted them to and prioritizing other things and people above me. It was painful, and I felt very neglected and sad about how their love and care for me shifted in another direction. Imagine how God feels when we become preoccupied in doing everything but communicate with him, everything but pray, everything but read his word, and everything but prioritize him in our lives.

God created us with the intention of communicating with us and having an intimate relationship with him. When God created Adam, prior to mankind's fall, he visited him in the Garden of Eden. God communed with Adam, he gave him a specific job to do (naming all the creatures), he saw the loneliness of his soul and created a help meet for him (Eve), and he gave him some dos and don'ts. "But of the fruit of the tree which is in the midst of the garden, God hath said, Ye shall not eat of it neither shall ye touch it, lest ye die" (Genesis 3:3).

God wanted Adam to avoid the penalty of death, so he warned him what not to do. This first glimpse of a parental and loving relationship between God and mankind is essential for the rest of us, for it reveals that God wants a loving and communicative relationship with us. In order to have a relationship with God, we must prioritize him in our life when we rise each day.

Who Do You Love the Most?

Have you gone to a restaurant or been in a public setting and noticed people sitting at a table or gathered in a group checking their smartphones for notifications, emails, and text messages? Cell phone pings or vibrations are continually going off, and hands are continually reaching for devices. We never want our cell phones too far from us throughout the day (do we). Have you ever accidentally left your cell phone at home and felt naked or loss without it? When this happened to me, it felt like I was not fully dressed without having it on me—near me. Wouldn't it be wonderful if we had that same desire for the Lord, in which we cannot be too far from him, we cannot be out of communication with him, we cannot miss a word from him for our lives, and we cannot neglect to interact with him each day!

If our desire for God exceeds, or even matches the same intensity that we have to interact with our technology devices each day, then the thirst to know him more would prevail in our lives. Stop the press! You may be thinking, "That is ridiculous! How can you compare our love for technology with our love for God?" Well, who (or what) are you giving more time to in your life? Love is not expressed merely by what we say, but it is shown by what we prioritize our time doing. It appears we have more consistency with responding to social media pages, games and apps than we do with spending time with God.

Bad Habits Can Be Broken

Bad habits are easy to form and hard to break. Bryant McGill wrote, "The secret to permanently breaking any bad habit is to love something greater than the habit". When we begin to love God more than the bad habit we allow to consume our time and energy, we will be empowered to grow. Ever decision we make, rings loudly of who we love more (God, self, money, fame, etc.). Our bad habits do not sneak up on us, but we practice and perfect them. Too often we practice godly habits sporadically and pick them back up again when faced with difficult times. This behavior keeps us on a merry-go-round of spiritual stagnation. Yet time keeps marching on day-after-day, week-after-week and year-after-year, and we are growing older and getting closer to our eternal destination. God is waiting for us to form godly habits, so we can become the light of the world and the salt of the earth (Matthew 5:13-16). God is not going to do what we are supposed to do in order to grow and mature in him, but we must do that for ourselves. God did all the necessary work on Calvary for us to be saved, but we must put in the work to stay saved when we rise each day. God's word guarantees us success if we follow his path for our lives.

The Voice of God

In order to know the voice of God, we must be familiar with how he sounds, how he speaks and how he reveals himself to us. It takes time to form a relationship with anyone. We spend time with people, and eventually become familiar with what pleases them, what annoys them, what things they are sensitive about, and what areas they are strong or weak in. A relationship with God works the same way. As we mature in God, we come to understand his nature. Equally so, we are glad God truly understands our human nature, our strengths and weaknesses, and he bears with us until we can walk in more victories than defeats. While this relationship is building, we are forming a habit of spending time with God and are getting to know him.

In order to replace a bad habit that is taking our attention and affection away from the Lord, we must be schooled in the word of God. Questions, such as these should be asked and answered: What pleases God? What does God require of me? What

can strengthen my relationship with the

behavior(s) will separate me from the Lord? Don't just think about these questions, and others, but plan how you will discover the answers, such as:

- Read the bible
- Attend church service regularly
- Confess your sins to God
- Repent from sin
- Have an accountability partner

Map out time each day when you can focus on God and are eagerly waiting to hear his voice and feel his presence. This is not difficult to do once you get thirsty enough for God and realize the relevance of prioritizing him in your daily lives.

My Technology Addiction

Some years ago, I became transfixed and addicted

to a game I downloaded on my cell phone and was giving way too much time and energy to it. I was feeding my cyber cows, pigs, chickens, goats, horses, dogs, cats, puppies and growing cyber crops several times a day. I was building up cyber farm houses, visiting cyber neighborhoods and purchasing cyber goods and products—rather than spending quality time with the Lord and working on pertinent things that needed my attention. I had really fallen into a technology stronghold!

My Bad Habit Replaced by Godly Habits

I deleted that game from my cell phone and planned to devote more time with God, which included: studying my bible, listening to various sermons at home, devoting time to listen to praise and worship songs, communicating and spending time with Christian friends, and joining church auxiliaries, etc. I haven't returned to that habitual, time-consuming habit again! Do you have to delete all the game apps from your cell phone or technology devices in order to spend quality time with God—of course not. I deleted one game app that I allowed to monopolize too much of my time and energy. I am glad I realized the enemy's ploy to divert my attention away from God, and I did something about it. I never want to go back to that robotic existence of playing a game several hours a day—while allowing my spiritual life to slip away and become stagnate. I was set free from that technology stronghold in my life. You, too, can be set free from the stronghold that is hindering you from maintaining a relationship with God.

Whatever is capturing your attention and affection, to the point that you have little to no time to spend with God, should be replaced by a godly habit that will draw you closer to the him. Don't just squeeze God in at the end of your busy day—after you have given your best efforts at work or on other activities—and are too exhausted to spend time with God. Set your alarm a little earlier in the morning, so when you rise each day, you can spend time with God.

Time Is Ticking

Geoffrey Chaucer said, "Time and tide wait for no man", and I wholeheartedly agree! When I was young, it felt as if time were my enemy, for it held me captive—due to my age—from doing what I wanted to do. What I wanted to do, as a thirteen-year old teenager growing up on the shores of Wildwood, New Jersey, was to go to the boardwalk at night and walk around with my friends as late as I wanted to. I imagined having no restrictions and making my own decisions for my life. However, mom knew I was too young and immature to handle that type of freedom, for I was unaware of all the dangers in the world that could happen to me if left unaccompanied by a loving and caring parent. Thank you, mom, for protecting me! Now that I am much older, time seems like an enemy pushing me faster than I want to go—roller coaster speed! There does not seem to be enough hours in a day to accomplish what I want, or need, to do. Weeks, months, and holidays are coming and going one-right-after-the-other, and there are no man-made brakes to slow down its pace.

Regardless of the season of life we are in, we are all living in God's timing. He is the creator of time and holds the blueprint for our life. If we yield ourselves to the Lord Jesus, he will reveal his plan for our lives. God told Jeremiah the prophet, "For I know the plans I have for you", declares the Lord, "plans to prosper you and not to harm you, plans to give you hope and a future" (Jeremiah 29:11 NIV). Those words had to be encouraging to Jeremiah, for he realized that God loved him, cared about his life, and had a unique plan that would assure him of a blessed future! Not only were those words meant for Jeremiah, but they are also meant for you and me. When the Lord created us, he created us for a purpose, to bless us, and guide us down a path toward a bright and hopeful future (isn't God good). God's purposeful path also includes being able to use us for his glory. All we need do is seek God's face, understand his will for us, and walk in his purpose. We don't have to worry about speeding up, or slowing down time, which we are totally incapable of doing anyway. When God blesses us to rise and greet a new day, spend time in his presence.

You have said, "Seek my face." My heart says to you, "Your face, Lord, do I seek."

Psalm 27:8 (ESV)

Questions:

1. The author wrote, "We sometimes see-saw between godly behaviors and old habits, which keeps us on a merry-go-round of spiritual stagnation." Has that ever happened to you? What is the danger of doing that?

2. The author wrote, "Our bad habits do not sneak up on us, but we practice and perfect them. "Is that true with every bad habit, or are we blindsided by some bad habits?

Questions:

3. Do you need to replace some bad habits in order to grow closer to the Lord? If so, what are they? What godly habits will you replace them with?

4. The author wrote, "We must make a conscious decision each day to spend quality time with God, so we can hear his voice and know his purpose for our lives." Do you spend quality time with God? If so, how has your life changed since doing that?

2

A MADE-UP MIND

Our bodies follow the trail of our thoughts. Before we do anything, we have already imagined what it looks like, what it feels like and how we will benefit from doing it. Franchise owners, marathon runners, Biggest Losers participants, Survivor contestants, and the Voice challengers imagined being able to overcome obstacles and gain the victory before they followed the trail of their thoughts.

The Apostle Paul painstakingly admonished the saints. He wrote, "Know ye not that ye are the temple of God, and that the spirit of God dwelleth in you" (1 Corinthians 3:16). Paul was evoking their memory of who they were supposed to be because some of them were following a trail of thoughts that led to un-Christlike behavior. Like the Corinthians, we too, will follow the trail of our thoughts if we do not have the mind of Christ.

Has an ungodly thought ever shot through your mind with an intensity comparable to lightning striking—and try to lodge there—so much so until you started rebuking the devil and calling on the name of Jesus? You knew you were not thinking thoughts like that a few minutes ago, and suddenly this crazy, lustful or ungodly thought pops into your mind.

The book of Revelation describes just how much

the enemy, Satan, works to separate us eternally from God. Even though he knows his destination has already been revealed in the word of God, as the Lake of Fire that burns for ever and ever (Revelation 20:10), it does not stop him from trying to deceive souls, so they too can be in eternal torment where he is going. Satan even tempted Jesus after his baptism in the Jordan River, and we are not above being tempted and tried like Jesus was. It's imperative, therefore, that we guard our souls by building up a consistent relationship with God. We need to have the mind of Christ, so that we can live victoriously and avoid eternal separation from God.

What does having the mind of Christ look like? The mind of Christ looks like a duplication of Christ's lifestyle and words. When Jesus Christ wrapped himself in flesh and came on the earth, he always said what God the Father said, and he always did what God the Father said to do. He became the duplicated divine nature of his heavenly Father—acted out upon the earth. As Christians, we should become the duplicated nature of Jesus Christ—acted out in our daily lives.

Jesus Did the Father's Will

Jesus was motivated by fulfilling God's will. In John 14:31, Jesus said, "But that the world may know that I love the Father; and as the Father gave me commandment, so I do. Arise, let us go hence." We must decide whether fulfilling God's will for our lives is more important than what we want to do. If we are not willing to exchange the position of "**my will**" to "**his will**", then we cannot be empowered for God's purpose. It's not that God does not want to empower us for his purpose, but we may not be allowing him to do it. Every decision we make and behavior we carry out reflects either our will or God's will being done in our life.

Jesus Said What the Father Said

"For I have not spoken of myself; but the Father which sent me, he gave me a commandment, what I should say, and what I should speak. And I know that his commandment is life everlasting: whatsoever I speak therefore, even as the Father said unto me, so I speak "(John 12:49-50). We must approach God with a humble spirit and be eager to hear from him. We must be willing to exchange our ideas and opinions for his, and in turn, he will trust us to speak what he says. Our opinions and ideas shouldn't contradict what is written in God's holy word, for God does not change with time, "Jesus Christ the same yesterday, and today, and forever" (Hebrews

13:8). In the scriptures throughout the old and new testament, we read where God communicates with his people; and because he is the same yesterday, today and forever more, that means he is still communicating with us in this present time. As he communicates his will for our lives, let us obey him, so that we can say what he tells us to say and do what he tells us to do—like Jesus did.

When Samuel the prophet was young, he was unfamiliar with the voice of the Lord. However, Eli the prophet instructed him how to respond the next time the Lord called his name, and he obeyed his instruction. Because of his obedience to Eli, he heard God's voice. "And the Lord came, and stood and called as at other times, Samuel, Samuel. Then Samuel answered, Speak; for thy servant heareth" (I Samuel 3:10).

When we are young in the Lord, we are not familiar with how God speaks, for we have no experience with hearing from him. As we grow in the Lord Jesus, we come to realize he speaks to our spirit through his written and spoken word. He speaks by affirming his will for our lives. He speaks by softly whispering to our spirit. When we are sensitive to knowing how God speaks, and can hear his voice, as in the case of Samuel, then we can say what God says and have confidence that it is the voice of the Lord speaking to us and through us.

Jesus Was Obedient to the Father

The most important characteristic that Jesus had was his willingness to always obey the Father's will. In John 8:29, Jesus said, "And he sent me is with me: the Father hath not left me alone; for I do always those things that please him." Jesus singularly, focused on obeying God's will—even when he would have preferred that the cup, he came to bear would be removed from him. "Saying, Father, if thou be willing, remove this cup from me: nevertheless not my will, but thine, be done" (Luke 22:42).

To be willingly crucified was the ultimate sacrifice of Jesus' obedience, which is seen in the following scriptures (Philippians 2:6-8):

> "Who, being in the form of God, thought it robbery to be equal with God. [7]But made himself of no reputation, and took upon him the form of a servant, and was made in the likeness of men. [8]And being found in fashion as a man, he humbled himself, and became obedient unto death, even the death of the cross."

Jesus felt the weight of his obedience as he prayed to the Father in the Garden of Gethsemane in

Matthew 26:38-39; 42 (ESV).

> [38]"Then he said to them, My soul is very sorrowful, even to death; remain here, and watch with me. [39]And going a little farther he fell on his face and prayed, saying, "My Father, if it be possible let this cup pass from me; nevertheless, not as I will, but as you will. [42]Again, for the second time, he went away and prayed, My Father if this cannot pass unless I drink it, your will be done."

If Jesus exchanged his will for the Father's will, we too must exchange our will for God's will. We must be willing to obey the word and follow the trail that leads to the purpose for which God created us. We should not expect that it will cost us nothing to obey God, when it cost Jesus his life to obey the Father. We must have a "made up mind" that whatever it takes, and wherever he leads us, we will obey God's will for our lives. We must be willing to be disliked or rejected by those who have settled for mediocrity in their walk with Christ, for we are reaching for godly perfection. "Not that I have already obtained it [this goal of being Christlike] or have already been made perfect, but I actively press on so that I may take hold of that [perfection] for which Christ Jesus took hold of me and made me his own" (Philippians 3:12 AMP). "Therefore, leaving the principles of the doctrine of Christ, let us go on unto perfection; not laying again the foundation of repentance from dead works, and of faith toward God" (Hebrews 6:1).

While in this earthly vessel, there will always be a struggle within us to obey God or obey our fleshly thoughts and desires. As we make decisions to obey the word of God—rather than the ungodly trails of our thoughts—we will begin to walk in more victories than defeats. We will be able to witness to others about how it is possible to overcome a stronghold in one's life, for through obedience and walking in God's will, we were able to overcome our strongholds. We will be a vessel that God can count on, that God can use for his glory, and that God is pleased with.

Remember how much God bragged on Job to Satan. God was so impressed by Job's continual obedience and prayers that he did not hold back his admiration. Now, I know none of us want to go through the severe testing that Job went through, but that shouldn't hold us back from striving for godly perfection and being willing to obey his word. Making up one's mind to have an intimate relationship with the Lord Jesus Christ is the "most important" decision you will make in this life, for its implications will be felt throughout all eternity. Since eternity outlasts our earthly years, decisions and actions which decide our eternal destination, are paramount to our spiritual well-being. Therefore, let us strive for godly perfection—not for mediocrity.

We won't give an account to God for anyone's decisions and behaviors but our own—regardless of our relationship with them. Therefore, let us focus solely on how we are walking, how we are talking and how we are living. Every time God allows us to rise and see a brand-new day that we have not seen before, we have been given an opportunity to strengthen our relationship with him (*praise God*). Waking-up mercies may not be there another day, so let's take advantage of the precious time God gives us. "It is of the Lord's mercies that we are not consumed, because his compassions fail not. They are new every morning: great is thy faithfulness" (Lamentations 3:22-23). "Remember what the bible says: Today when you hear his voice, don't harden your hearts as Israel did when they rebelled" (Hebrews 3:15 NLT).

When we decide that loving and serving God is the most important thing in this world to us, then the trail of that thought will lead us down a path of spiritual victory!

Questions:

1. Is spiritual mediocrity easy to recognize in others and difficult to recognize in ourselves? If so, why?

2. Is your mind made up to exchange your will for God's will? If not, what is holding you back from fully committing yourself and yielding to his will for your life?

Questions:

3. Do you remember the first time you heard the Lord's voice? Is God's voice still drawing you closer to him? If so, are you striving to obey his voice and purpose for your life?

4. The author spoke about guarding our souls? How are you guarding your soul from Satan's destructive strategies?

3

SPIRITUAL DEAL BREAKERS

What are your spiritual deal breakers? I love to watch the shows on HGTV. Singles and married couples usually have an idea of what they will, or will not, accept in a house they want to purchase. Things, such as: the number of bedrooms, number of bathrooms, a man-cave, an open concept floor plan, adequate yard space, and the location of the house are extremely important to them. If a house is almost perfect, but it lacks the one thing that they must have, they will not purchase it, for the deal breaking component was missing, and the house hunting continues. Just like those who are seeking their perfect house, whether it's a starter home or a mansion, we too are particular about what we want, where we want it, and what condition we will accept it in. However, the one criterion, that will allow us to get what we want is always determined by the size of our budget we have. Our aspirations and desires can be on a grand scale, but if our budget is not, we must settle for what our budget will allow us to purchase. The deal breaker then shifts into a state of compromise.

Just like a house hunter's deal breaker can be shifted into a state of compromise due to a lack of budget, we too can be shifted into a state of spiritual compromise by a lack of commitment to God. It is imperative, therefore, that we establish spiritual deal breakers, so that we will not compromise our morals, ethical behavior, and righteous living in order to achieve riches, relationships, and positions in this life.

As Christians, we must decide what we will, or will not, do or accept in our walk with Christ. If we want to walk in **integrity**, then our spiritual deal breaker should be to resist and reject untruths and dishonest behavior. In Colossians 3:9 (NIV), it states, "Do not lie to each other, since you have taken off your old self with its practices." Telling the truth, affirming the truth and walking in the truth brings honor to God and yourself. An honorable and truthful reputation will not only gain you favor with God—but with mankind also.

If we want **self-control**, then our spiritual deal breaker should be to resist and reject promiscuous and unrestrained behavior that is not like Christ. "No temptation has overtaken you except what is common to mankind. And God is faithful; he will not let you be tempted beyond what you can bear. But when you are tempted, he will also provide a way out so that you can endure it" (1 Corinthians 10:13 NIV). In 1 Corinthians 6:12 (NLT), it states, "You say, "I am allowed to do anything"—but not everything is good for you. And even though "I am allowed to do anything," I must not become a slave to anything". When opportunities and offers come our way that will place us in positions of yielding to temptations, we must do like Joseph did in the bible (Genesis 39:1-12) and remove ourselves from the situation—run if you have too!

If we want **love**, then our spiritual deal breaker should be to resist and reject every unjust, unkind, and unloving thought, feeling and action that attempts to bring destruction to others and ourselves. In John 13:34-35, it states, [34] "A new commandment I give unto you, That ye love one another; as I have loved you, that ye also love one another. [35]By this shall all men know that ye are my disciples, if ye have love one to another." In 1 John 4:11, it states "Beloved, if God so loved us, we ought also to love one another."

If we want to be an **encourager of others** (and ourselves), then our spiritual deal breaker should be to control what comes out of our mouths. "Set a watch, O LORD, before my mouth; keep the door of my lips" (Psalm 141:3). In Proverbs 18:21, it states, "Death and life are in the power of the tongue: and they that love it shall eat the fruit thereof."

You get the idea now! If we want to rise each day in victory, we must know who we are, whose we are, what we will accept, what we won't accept, and what we are striving to obtain in God. We don't haphazardly fall into victorious living without first planning on how we will achieve it.

The Holy Bible is God's blueprint of himself, which allows us to gain an understanding of how we should live. The reason we needed a savior was that we were in an unsaved state doing whatever came to our minds, and therefore, we followed the trail of our thoughts continually. Some of our thoughts were good and pleasant and yielded good results, but many of our thoughts were sinful, and that nature ruled our flesh and controlled our behavior. "Behold, I was born a sinner—yes, from the moment my mother conceived me" (Psalm 51:5 NLT).

Prior to becoming a Christian, we made New Year Resolutions, year-after-year, but lacked the power to walk in all our good intentions. We cannot keep our spiritual deal breakers without God's help and power in our lives, "….for without me ye can do nothing" (John 15:5). When opportunities are presented to us, we should remember the spiritual deal breakers we established to keep us on the path of righteousness and spiritual growth. If an opportunity will bless us financially but hinder our spiritual walk with Christ—for it keeps us out of the house of God on a regular basis, keeps us from spending quality time with God, keeps us from spending quality time with our families, or requires that we compromise our moral and ethical standards—then the cost is too high! We should walk away from those opportunities. Some opportunities camouflage themselves as blessings, however, they separate you from serving God. If we are thirsty enough for God, it will be difficult to separate us from God. The question that should be explored then is how thirsty are you for God? How bad do you want to know God? Are you willing to exchange your priorities, so that your life mimics God? Every decision we make reveals our thirst level for God. Our decisions reveal whether we are about serving him or whether we are serving our personal ambitions. Our decisions speak loudly, for our behavior follows the trail of our thoughts.

O God, thou art my God; early will I seek thee: my soul thirtieth for thee, my flesh longed for thee in a dry and thirsty land, where no water is;

(Psalm 63:1)

Questions:

1. The author stated, "Some opportunities camouflage themselves as blessings, however, they separate you from serving God." Have you recognized camouflaged opportunities in your life? If so, what did you do about them?

2. What does your priorities reveal about you?

Questions:

3. The author wrote," We don't haphazardly fall into victorious living without first planning on how we will achieve it?" Have you planned to walk in victory with God? If so, what did you do?

4. Do you have spiritual deal breakers that keep spiritual boundaries secure in your life? If so, what are they?

4

HOW THIRSTY ARE YOU?

Thirst has different levels and can be felt in various areas of our lives. On a hot summer day when the sun's rays are beaming down on you, your thirst needs to be quenched immediately. When your bills exceed your income, a thirst for more money lights an ignition in you to look for a second stream of income. When you are in your mid 30s and still unmarried, the thirst to say, "I Do", may influence you to re-evaluate what you will, or will not, accept in a potential spouse. An unquenched thirst is a frustrating feeling. The desire to have something that seems unattainable can play with our emotions and influence our decisions. According to James 4:2 (NLT) it states,

> "You want what you don't have, so you scheme and kill to get it. You are jealous of what others have, but you can't get it so you fight and wage war to take it away from them. Yet you don't have what you want because you don't ask God for it".

Every thirst is not ungodly or won't lead us into unholy living, but the greatest thirst we should strive to quench is our thirst to be like Jesus. "Blessed are those who hunger and thirst for righteousness, for they will be filled" (Matthew 5:6 NIV).

In John 4, a Samaritan woman approached

Jacob's well in Sychar, preparing to draw water, and Jesus asked her for a drink. His request surprised her, for she recognized him as being a Jew, and the Jews had no dealings with Samaritans at that time. The woman talked about the history of the well. She asked Jesus if he were greater than their father Jacob, which gave them the well and drank from it himself, his children and cattle. Jesus answered, "Everyone who drinks this water will be thirsty again, but whoever drinks the water I give them will never thirst. Indeed, the water I give them will become in them a spring of water welling up to eternal life" (John 4:13-14 NIV).

Jesus addressed the Samaritan woman's thirst for love and acceptance, for she had had five husbands, and the man she was with now was not her husband. Jesus did not dwell on her past or present circumstances, but he let her know "yet a time is coming, and has now come, when the true worshippers will worship the Father in the Spirit and truth, for they are the kind of worshippers the Father seeks" (John 4:23 NIV). That one conversation with Jesus turned her into a street evangelist, in which she proclaimed him to be the Messiah. "Many of the Samaritans from that town believed in him because of the woman's testimony, He told me everything I ever did" (John 4:39-40 NIV). One touch from God or one word whispered to our souls is enough to set us ablaze with renewed passion and fire to run on in Jesus name!

As we strive to quench our thirst for more of God, more of his presence, more of his understanding, more of his knowledge, more of his power, and more of his love—we will find that our thirst in other areas of our lives are being worked out according to the timing and will of God. Nothing then is more important than being with him, feeling him in our lives, and fulfilling the purpose for which he created us. In John 6:35, Jesus promised to quench our hunger and thirst for him, he said, "I am the bread of life; he that cometh to me shall never hunger; and he that believeth on me shall never thirst." God has promised to satisfy our thirst for more of him. In Matthew 5:6 (NIV), he said, "Blessed are those who hunger and thirst for righteousness, for they shall be filled."

When God makes a promise, it must come to pass. "God is not man, that he should lie, or a son of man, that he should change his mind. Has he said, and will he not do it? Or has he spoken, and will not he fulfill it" (Numbers 23:19 ESV). So, if our thirst is not being quenched by God, then there is a problem with our thirst level—not with the ability of God to satisfy it.

As the deer pants for the water brooks, So pants my soul for You, O God. My soul thirsts for God, for the living God. When shall I come and appear before God?

Psalm 42:1-2 (NKJV)

Questions:

1. The author wrote, "An unquenched thirst is a frustrating feeling. The desire to have something that seems unattainable can play with our emotions and influence our decisions." Do you remember a time like that in your life? How was it resolved?

2. Are you thirsty for God? Does it show in what you pursue? If so, how?

Questions:

3. Has God ever spoken a word to you that put everything into perspective? If so, how did it change your life?

4. We don't have wells to boast about—as the Samaritan woman did. However, do we place too much emphasis on things that are less important than our relationship with God? If so, what are some of those things?

5

WALKING IN THE VALLEY WITH GOD

I once saw a movie, *A River Runs Through It*. The characters included a Presbyterian minister, his wife and two sons—one was scholarly (Norman), and the other was free-spirited (Paul). It was interesting and endearing watching how the father and sons spent quality time in their favorite spot along the river—fly fishing. They learned to cast using a ticking metronome, and the boys become accomplished fishermen. You could see the admiration they had for one another as they swung their fishing lines rhythmically through the air, back-and-forth, until they cast their line into a deep part of the river—expecting it to yield a nice-size trout. The film cleverly drew its viewers in as the relationship between the family unfolded and the seasons of life changed for then all.

Paul's fishing skills developed far beyond that of his father and brother, and Norman realized who was truly the master of fly fishing when he came home to visit. However, Paul also developed an addictive gambling habit while Norman was away at college. The innocent season when they were boys was over, and in Pauls' case, it was replaced by gambling (and other vices). We saw (and felt) Paul's downward spiral—as did his brother Norman. As we watched the movie, we hoped Paul would be delivered from his gambling addiction. It was painful watching what

Paul had become, and our emotions escalated more knowing he associated with gamblers who didn't tolerate running up too much debt—and Paul was maxed out in gambling debts. Paul was in a dark valley in his life, but he didn't seem to want to be delivered from it. Norman was disturbed about Paul's behavior, but Paul rejected his help. The climax of the movie occurred when Norman received a phone call from the police telling him that Paul was found beaten to death in an alley. There was no happy ending for Paul in the movie, and Norman's heart-felt desire for his brother to be delivered from his destructive behavior was not realized.

We all go through valley seasons in our lives when it seems as though the severity of the trial, test and conflict was orchestrated to suck the joy, hope and very life out of our soul—at least it can feel like that. Valley seasons uncover our weaknesses and allow us to become acquainted with a side of our character that was hidden below the surface until the right amount of pressure revealed it. Somewhere amid the pain, sorrow, anger and frustration, our focus shifts to our inner self where we begin to travail, pray and plead for deliverance, peace and victory. We then are no longer consumed with "why", but we want help in the time of trouble. "Though he slay me, yet will I trust in him" (Job 13:15). Valley experiences have a way of humbling us, so that we are receptive to hearing what God has to say and are willing to yield to it. We become seekers of God in the valley.

Like in the movie, *A River Runs Through It*, some valley experiences don't end the way we want them to. Have you ever prayed, fasted and believed God for a miracle for yourself, a family member, a co-worker or friend, and the direct opposite happened? Inwardly, you have this conversation with yourself and God about how you thought your prayer would be answered as you visualized it. You may even question whether your faith was strong enough, whether you were empowered enough for God to work a miracle through you, or whether you could have done more to prevent the story from ending that way.

I found myself asking these questions when my mother died from cancer June 22, 2016. I wondered if I were stronger spiritually, then perhaps God could have used me to lay hands on her, and she miraculously would have recovered. I had a conversation with God for two days after mom died about this—accompanied with the feelings of guilt that I could have done more. I felt if I was empowered like the apostles in the book of Acts, then even if mom died, God could have worked through me to raise her from the dead. I even felt foolish to express these thoughts to anyone, for I wasn't sure how they would be received from the hearer, and so I worked through confusing conversations in my mind daily. God spoke to me on my way home after viewing mom's body the day before the funeral service. I pulled up to a red light playing the same conversation over-and-over again in my mind, and God said to me, "**Count Your Blessings**!". In other words, God wanted me to focus on the fact that I was blessed for having had a loving, Christian mother for 82 years. He wasn't going to give me an explanation why he called her home when he did. He wasn't going to explain why he chose not to use me to lay hands on her, so that she could recover. Rather, God gave me words that helped me to recover from not understanding his will for my mother. After God said, "Count Your Blessings", my perspective shifted from that moment on. I exchanged my questioning God and asking him "why" to "thanking" him for allowing me and my siblings to have had her in our lives for as long as we did. God was merciful to me, for I could have continued to mull over those questions again-and-again for weeks and months, which would have led to emotional torment. God delivered me by speaking three words in my heart. A year after my mother's death, I was able to finish and publish the journal I started writing when I was with her during her last week on earth. Writing has always been a means of releasing my emotions, and I needed to get them out somehow. My book, *A Journal of My*

Last Week with Mom, has been a blessing to those who knew her and to those who are going through a death journey experience with their loved one.

Sometimes during valley experiences, we want to appear stronger than what we are feeling because we do not want to be perceived as a weak Christian. There are, however, some valleys that render us speechless and tears are the fountain of our release. After all, God created tears for them to flow—didn't he? At some point; though, we must allow God's Holy Spirit to comfort us in his love—even if we don't understand, "why" something happened—and rise again. "Who comforts us in all of our troubles, so that we can comfort those in any trouble with the comfort we ourselves receive from God "(2 Corinthians 1:4 NIV). Another beautiful valley scripture is, "You came near when I called you; you said, "Do not fear" (Lamentations 3:57 ESV).

We must rely upon the grace of God to see us through every situation—as the Apostle Paul did in 2 Corinthians 12:9, "My grace is sufficient for thee: for my strength is made perfect in weakness. Most gladly therefore will I rather glory in my infirmities, that the power of Christ may rest upon me." Admitting there are times in our lives when we need an abundant level of strength and comfort from God to see us through, humanizes our Christian walk and makes us relatable to others. As in the following scripture, we derive much joy in the fact that we serve a God that can feel our pain and insecurities, and he empathizes with what we are going through.

"For we do not have a high priest who is unable to empathize with our weaknesses, but we have one who has been tempted in every way, just as we are-yet he did not sin. Let us then approach God's throne of grace with confidence, so that we may receive mercy and find grace to help us in our time of need" (Hebrews 4:15-16 ESV).

Job faced a horrendous valley in his life. 'The bible describes Job as being blameless and upright— who feared God and shunned evil. Early in the morning, he would sacrifice burnt offerings for each of his children, thinking, "Perhaps my children have sinned and cursed God in their hearts". This was Job's regular custom" (Job 1:5 NIV). Even though Job lived a righteous life, his seven sons and three daughters were killed. Job's servants were killed— except the ones who escaped to tell him what happened. Job's sheep, camels, oxen and donkeys were either destroyed or stolen, and the one remaining family member suggested Job curse God and die (Job 2:9). Imagine this happening on the same day—in quick succession one right behind one another. Yet, job declared, "Though he slay me, yet will I trust in him" (Job 13:15).

There is no way to avoid valley experiences. Regardless of whether we pray daily, fast weekly, or attend church service regularly—we will all go through valley experiences. We must purposely prepare for life by remaining close to Jesus. By doing so, we will be able to go through valley experiences that come in our lives. God brings us out of our valley experiences in his timing (not ours), and we will rise again! "But they that wait upon the Lord shall renew their strength, they shall mount up with wings as eagles; they shall run, and not be weary; and they shall walk, and not faint" (Isaiah 40:31).

Questions:

1. The author wrote, "Sometimes during valley experiences, we want to appear stronger than what we are feeling because we do not want to be perceived as a weak Christian". Have you ever felt like that before?

2. The author wrote, "Valley seasons uncover our weaknesses and allow us to become acquainted with a side of our character that was hidden below the surface until the right amount of pressure revealed it." Has this ever happened to you?

Questions:

3. The author wrote, "After all, God created tears for them to flow—didn't he?" Are tears a healing ointment for you when you go through a valley experience? If not, what is?

4. Walking by faith is not always easy in a valley experience, but it's possible for our faith to rebound. What was the hardest valley experience you went through, and how did you hold onto, or rebound, with renewed faith?

6

EXPOSED FOR OUR GOOD

Exposure awakens others to an awareness of facts that were hidden from the eyes of the general public—far beneath the surface. Exposure is like a white flag being waved through the air, which gains the attention of onlookers. It's like a bullhorn that was unexpectedly turned on, so now everyone clearly hears the message that was meant to be kept secret.

In the book of Ecclesiastes, we read where everything has a season, and there is a time to every purpose under heaven (Ecclesiastes 3:1). Exposure has a set time when it will burst forth suddenly, and without warning, reveal hidden secrets, sinful behaviors, and immoral deeds. Exposure is held captive by mercy and grace for a time period—not forever, though!

Prior to accepting Jesus Christ as our Lord and Savior, we were practicing sinners who were accustomed to living life our own way. We governed our own footsteps. God gives us time to change from our old lifestyles and habits to our new nature.

How Soon We Forget

When the prophet Nathan told King David about his sin, he didn't recognize himself. Nathan illustrated his sin by telling a story.

"Then Nathan said to David, "You are that rich man! This is what the Lord, the God of

Israel, says: "I chose you to be the king of Israel. I saved you from Saul. I let you take his family and his wives, and I made you king of Israel and Judah. As if that had not been enough, I would have given you more and more. So why did you ignore my command? Why did you do what I say is wrong? You let the Ammonites kill Uriah the Hittite, and you took his wife. It is as if you yourself killed Uriah in war" (2 Samuel 12:7-9 ESV).

Yes, this was the same King David that worshipped God openly in the streets, that fought and defeated Goliath, the giant, and prevailed against God's enemies in battle. Yet, his desire for Bathsheba, another man's wife, was so great that he fell into a state of masking the right for the wrong until God's prophet was sent to openly uncover his sin by way of exposing what he had done. Exposing David's sin did not have to take place if he had yielded under mercy and grace, repented from committing adultery with Bathsheba, and recommitted his life to God. However, he tried to make permanent what was not his from the beginning by having Bathsheba's husband killed. He and Bathsheba felt joyful about the expectant delivery of their unborn child—not taking into consideration the great price Uriah paid for their newfound happiness. Therefore, mercy and grace took a temporary leave of absence, so judgement and justice could be executed for their sin.

We later read the punishment that God exacts unto David,

[10] "So your family will never have peace!

When you took Uriah's wife, you showed that you did not respect me." [11]" This is what the Lord says: 'I am bringing trouble against you. This trouble will come from your own family. I will take your wives from you and give them to someone who is very close to you. He will have sexual relations with your wives, and everyone will know it!" [12] "You had sexual relations with Bathsheba in secret, but I will punish you so that all the people of Israel can see it."

[13]Then David said to Nathan, "I have sinned against the Lord." Nathan said to David, "The Lord will forgive you, even for this sin. You will not die. [14]"But you did things that made the Lord's enemies lose their respect for him, so your new baby son will die." (2

Samuel 12:10, 12-14 ERV).

God forgave David, but he still was punished. His sin was exposed for all to see, but he did **rise again**! God alone decides when corrective actions should be initiated in our lives. He alone decides what methods should be used to get our attention, so we like David can confess and repent from our sin(s). Those who have been exposed, seem to have one thing in common—the desire to turn back the hand of time and stop it at the onset.

We are grateful for the grace and mercy of God in our lives, and we can readily recall a time (numerous times in fact) when we should have been exposed and received punishment instead of God's mercy and grace. There is a saying that is popular among Christians today, which is "anything or anyone attached to me wins". However, when exposure takes place, it's good to remember, "anything or anyone attached to me is shamed". Exposure, therefore, not only affects our personal life, but it affects our spouse, our children, our loved ones, our friends, our church, our business—anything or anyone that is attached to us!

Let's Be Honest, Shall We

There were (are) times in our life when we knew (know) what God's word says, yet we wanted (want) what we wanted (want)—and we did (do) it anyhow (anyway). But God is loving, patient and forgiving toward us. His love and patience have a purpose; "And remember, our Lord's patience gives people time to be saved" (2 Peter 3:15 NLT). God gives us time to work things out in our lives that are not yielded to his word and will. "….work out your own salvation with fear and trembling" (Philippians 2:12).

No one wants to be embarrassed, but when we are not willing to obey God's word—when given ample opportunities to do so—exposure becomes necessary for God to help keep us on the path of salvation. "The Lord is not slack concerning his promise, as some men count slackness; but is longsuffering to usward, not willing that any should perish, but that all should come to repentance" (2 Peter 3:9).

Exposure brings a clarity to one's mind that starts an inner evaluation of one's deeds. It forces us to reflect upon our actions and come to terms with what we have done. The pleasure and joy that was derived from the sinful behavior seems to dissipate when exposure takes place. The character trait of integrity begins to develop once again. Even though others may not know what we do when no one is looking—like in the game of peekaboo—God can see us when we slip out of his will. God has the power to search the reigns of our hearts like no one can. "I the LORD search the heart and examine the mind, to reward each person according to their conduct, according to what their deeds deserve" (Jeremiah 17:10 NIV). We then cry out "Create in me a clean heart, O God and renew a right spirit within me" (Psalm 51:10 ESV).

Exposure is then a tool the Lord uses to draw us closer to him—when necessary. As parents, we use different types of methods to teach our children what we want them to learn—especially our children who are stubborn and rebellious. We don't just speak the type of behavior we want modeled in our children, but we model the behavior ourselves and have consequences in place—just in case they choose to disregard our words and life-living example and do what they want to do anyway (anyhow). God, our heavenly Father, does the same thing. He speaks to us through his written word, preached word and to our hearts about what type of behavior we should have. The only thing he doesn't provide us with is a desire and willingness to obey him. We must supply that for ourselves.

Even when our sin is exposed by God, we can **rise again** through repentance and obedience—like David did. There is no level you can sink to where God cannot pull you back up from. Our relationship with God can be restored, and we can be made whole once again.

Questions:

1. Exposure is not an easy thing to endure. Have you ever been exposed before? If so, how did you recover?

2. If you've ever been exposed and recovered, what advice would you give someone else experiencing that?

Questions:

3. Is it harder to deal with our sin or to keep it hidden? Why?

4. Describe what you felt like when you were bound in sin but overcame it with God's help? Are you still free from that sin?

7

THE ROAD TO RECOVERY

Coming out of a bound situation is an exhilarating feeling—comparable to a wounded eagle who is now able to take flight again. The eagle feels the wind of freedom soaring through its wings, sees new possibilities on the horizon, and is restored to its former glory. When we are brought back into fellowship with God, we are joyful and grateful for God's forgiveness, have a different perspective on our walk with Christ, and are determined not to repeat the behavior that led us down the path of separation from God. In Micah 7: 18-19 (NIV), it states,

"[18]Who is a God like you, who pardons sin and forgives the transgression of the remnant of his inheritance? You do not stay angry forever but delight to show mercy. [19] You will again have compassion on us; you will tread our sins underfoot and hurl all our iniquities into the depths of the sea."

When we think about a time when we went to someone and asked for forgiveness, wanted forgiveness, but forgiveness was withheld from us—we can see how far and wide God's love, mercy and forgiveness is from ours. Even when we have grown in the Lord Jesus, there is just no comparing our level of love, mercy and forgiveness with Gods.

The parable of the prodigal son (Luke 15:11-32), tells of a younger son who had become disgruntled with the mundane routine of his life. Rather than wait until he inherited his portion from his father, he asked for his inheritance prematurely. He abandoned his father, and the responsibilities he had as a son, to follow the trail of his thoughts and desires. Least any of us forget where the trail of our thoughts carried us before Jesus restored us back into fellowship, Ephesians 2:2-3 sums it up,

> [2]" Wherein in the time past ye walked according to the course of this world, according to the prince of the power of the air, the spirit that now worketh in the children of disobedience. [3]Among whom also we all had our conversation in times past in the lusts of our flesh, fulfilling the desires of the flesh and of the mind; and were by nature the children of wrath, even as others. "

The prodigal son desired to experience life without the restraints of his father's influence. He wanted to do his own thing. He wanted freedom to choose. What he didn't realize is that he was leaving the environment of a loving father who had restrictions in place to help him avoid the entrapments, enticements, and sins that come from indulging in the world's pleasures. Upon his request, though, the father gave him his inheritance, and he gathered all his things and took a journey to a far country. Like the prodigal son's father, our heavenly father will not force us to remain in his word or will if we insist on living life our way. God gives us the freedom to choose whom we will serve.

Our behavior is curtailed when we are in a familiar environment among familiar people, who judge our unrestrained behavior for what it is—sin!

Therefore, the desire to get as far away as possible from people who know we should be behaving according to what we were taught, propels us to put some distance from them.

According to the bible, the prodigal son wasted his "substance with riotous living" (Luke 15:13). His newfound freedom, however, was short-lived when a severe famine rose up in that country, and he had nothing to live on. His attempt to solve his unemployment was to become a citizen of that country, but he was given a lowly position—feeding swine. Prior to leaving his father, he was in a position of authority—his father having servants in his house. Now, he had been reduced to feeding swine in a foreign country that did not know him nor recognize his position of sonship. When we behave in an adverse manner that does not reflect what we are and who we are, we will not be recognized as a child of our heavenly father.

God didn't allow the prodigal son's employment to bail him out of his current predicament. He allowed his stomach to growl with hunger. He allowed his friends to ignore his plight. He allowed him to be humiliated. The prodigal son had sunken so far down in his life that he ate the same food he fed the swine. He was no longer dinning like a son, who benefited from his father's provisions.

When we do not deserve to be blessed because of our sin, because of our rebellion and because of our unsteadfastness, God still says, "Casting all your care upon him; for he careth for you" (I Peter 5:7). Even when we become someone that others do not love, do not want and reject, God embraces us with his longsuffering and open arms—called another chance. God's love and forgiveness gives us the confidence to call out to him for mercy, so we can experience his bountiful grace and be restored.

Transformation begins when we become aware that we are nothing without God in our lives. Clarity takes hold of our wrapped thinking, and we realize that the contrary trails of our thoughts led us down a path of destruction. The prodigal son began to transform his thinking. He remembered his experience in his father's house. He remembered how his father treated him as a son. He remembered the comfort and plentiful provisions he had the privilege of having whenever he needed something.

"[17]And when he came to himself, he said, How many hired servants of my father's have bread enough and to spare, and I perish with hunger! [18]I will arise and go to my father, and will say unto him, Father, I have sinned against heaven, and before thee. [19]And am no more worthy to be called thy son: make me as one of thy hired servants" (Luke 15:17-19).

His transformed mind propelled him into action. "And he arose, and came to his father" (Luke 15:20). With each footstep toward his father, the prodigal son was relying on his father's goodness. He was relying on his father's mercy and grace. He wanted to be accepted back—even if it meant he would not be restored to his original position of sonship. He walked toward his father's direction hoping and praying. He walked and discovered the power of prayer during his journey back home. As each footstep took him closer and closer to his destination, he pictured the warm embrace of his father's acceptance. No more eating swine food. No more dwelling in a strange country, where no one came to his aid and did not care whether he lived or died. He was heading to a place of love, comfort and provision. He kept walking and found that his father's love didn't diminish with time—it was as if he had never gone away. The father rejoiced at his return, and the son was loved, embraced and restored to sonship—where he belonged!

Like the prodigal son, the road to recovery for all of us is possible, for God declares in his word, "Turn, O blacksliding children, saith the LORD; for I am married unto you" (Jeremiah 3:14).

Repentance starts with us coming to ourselves, in which we clearly see our sinful state and desire to change. I am so glad that God restores, revives, and renews our souls when it seems like all hope is gone. The prodigal son wanted to return home to his father. When we desire to return to our heavenly father after we fall, he is right there with his arms open wide to receive us back again. We rejoice at the comforting words in Matthew 11:28-29: [28]"Come to me, all of you who are weary and burdened, and I will give you rest. [29] Take up my yoke and learn from me, because I am lowly and humble in heart, and you will find rest for your souls."

We have relatives, classmates, friends, or co-workers that may have loved and served God at one time in their life, but they fell back into a lifestyle of sin. There are many complicated situations in our society, but we know God can restore those who want to be brought back into fellowship with him. Just like God helped us rise from ungodly behavior and situations in our lives, he can do the same for them.

Questions:

1. The author wrote, "God didn't allow the prodigal son's employment to bail him out of his current predicament." Were there times in your life when your abilities and talents didn't bail you out of a bad situation? If so, how did you come out of it?

2. The author wrote, "Transformation begins when we become aware that we are nothing without God in our lives." How sobering was that realization to you, and how did it affect your behavior and decisions?

Questions:

3. The author wrote, "Even when we become someone that others do not love, do not want and reject, God embraces us with his longsuffering and open arms—called another chance." How important is this to remember when we deal with others who offend and disappoint us?

4. The Author wrote, "The father rejoiced at his return, and the son was restored to sonship—where he belonged!" Is there a state in which we are in "limbo" (not saved or unsaved)? Explain.

8

PERSEVERE THROUGH IT ALL

In 2 Peter 3:18, it states, "But grow in grace, and in the knowledge of our Lord and Savior Jesus Christ. To him be glory both now and forever." In Matthew, Mark, Luke and John, we see how the disciples matured spiritually from when they were initially called by Jesus to follow him on his earthy ministry—to when they were scattered from the Garden of Gethsemane. The disciples were immediately thrust into independency when Jesus was taken in the

Garden of Gethsemane. Every spoken word Jesus said to them prior to that moment, every healing that took place, every demon that was cast out, every response Jesus gave to the religious sect of that day who challenged his authority would now have to be replayed over-and-over again in their hearts and minds, for they would have to walk their Christian life without him by their side from now on. Jesus prepared the disciples for this day. He warned them that he would be going away shortly. He taught them about the god-like nature they should have, and equally important he demonstrated godliness by his behavior every day he spent in their presence. Even in the Garden of Gethsemane, during a moment he would have preferred not to endure, he healed a high priest's ear that Peter cut off. In so doing, Jesus demonstrated that whatever we go through, we should not be totally consumed with just what we are dealing with. We should respond to others who need help and need to be ministered to.

The purpose for which Jesus came to earth was being played out before him in the Garden of Gethsemane. Jesus would soon be brought before religious leaders and questioned about his purpose, witnesses would lie on him, and he would be ridiculed by those who had a mission to destroy him (or so they thought). Jesus was standing on the threshold of receiving a beating so severe that the prophet Isaiah described it in 52:14 (NLT), "But many were amazed when they saw him. His face was so disfigured he seemed hardly human, and from his appearance, one would scarcely know he was a man."

There are times in our lives when problems, oppositions, trials and temptations come at us in waves—like a wave crashing against the seashore. When that sudden shift takes place in the atmosphere of our lives, we find ourselves in a persevere mode. How we go through these moments in our lives, sends an unspoken message to onlookers about how connected we are to God. When we are in control of our emotions, our words, and behavior during severe testing, we leave behind the fragrance of Jesus, which is holiness.

However, sometimes it can be challenging to control our emotions, when what we believe in and stand for is challenged, attacked or questioned, especially today where right behavior is looked upon as being wrong, and wrong behavior is looked upon as being right. Regardless of how the world's standards fluctuate, we must persevere to be like Jesus in words and deeds. We must hold onto God's standards of right and wrong—even when it seems we are singularly standing alone in our belief.

As Christians, we should not go around offending others and not care whether we evoke negative emotions in others due to what we are feeling at the time. Peter allowed his emotions to control his actions when he cut off the high priest servant's ear in the Garden of Gethsemane, but Jesus emotions were so controlled and yielded to God the Father that he cared more about what was happening to someone else than what he was getting ready to endure. As a result, he reattached and healed his ear.

Having self-control over our body, mouth, and behavior is an indication of spiritual growth. Growth does not happen overnight. Like in the lives of the disciples who continued to grow spiritually and mature after Jesus resurrection, we should be evolving into being more-and-more like Jesus in our lives. We should mature to the point where we care just as much about our responses and actions as we do about what we are going through. Jesus earthly ministry has already been completed, and he has placed us in this moment and time to let others know who Jesus is through us. Severe testing and temptations are but for a season (like in Job's life), but the trace of our actions linger on in the memory of onlookers for a long time.

It's easy to allow the love of God to flow through our lives and minister to others when we are being loved, being treated with respect and honor, and everything is going well in our lives, but can we love others, respect others, and minister to others when we are being opposed and mistreated—that's the time when perseverance is needed.

It is easy to revert to our sinful nature and allow profanity to flow, evil thoughts to lodge in our mind, and our behavior to offend others. However, it takes great strength and perseverance to control our actions and love others when they are difficult to love. When we think about our past, and how we fulfilled the lusts of our flesh, but then God's grace and mercy embraced us until we began to change (and are still changing) into his image—we should be patient with others. In Matthew 18:21 Peter asked, "Lord, how oft shall my brother sin against me, and I forgive him? till seven times?". Jesus responded, "I say not unto thee, Until seven times: but, Until seventy times seven" (Matthew 18:22). In other words, we do not get to a certain point, and say to someone, "you've maxed out on forgiveness with me, so now I can hold a grudge". I have seen many Facebook posts like this,

"Once you lose my forgiveness, you will never get it back!" I'm so glad that Jesus does not cut us off as easily as we do others when they offend us!

Persevering to be like Jesus is understanding the very nature of God and sincerely striving to be like him—regardless what trials come our way. One characteristic of Jesus nature is to forgive others, so they can be restored back into fellowship with God and mankind. Rather than merely singing the song, "Just to Be Like Jesus", let us strive to be like Jesus.

Just as Jesus cried out to the Father in the Garden of Gethsemane and asked if it were possible that this cup (assignment) be taken from him, knowing the painful things that were going to happen to him, we must also cry out to God daily asking him to help us to persevere, so he can be glorified through us each morning **When We Rise!**

When We Rise

Questions:

1. Have you ever reached your maximum forgiveness level with someone, and then you had to persevere to forgive again and treat them with God's love? If so, how did you get through that ordeal?

2. How do you re-focus when you must persevere?

Questions:

3. What situation comes to mind that reminds you about how much God forgave you for something? Does that thought help you forgive others?

4. Is there any situation that God cannot help us persevere through? If not, then is there any reason we can give for not making it to heaven?

PATRICIA DABOH is the author of, *A Journey of My Last Week with Mom*. She is an evangelist, humanitarian, nonprofit consultant, and the Founder of a charitable, nonprofit organization entitled, *The Remnant Seekers, Inc.* Her nonprofit organization serves the homeless community in Greensboro, North Carolina and co-sponsors tiny houses for them to live. She's the mother of six children, nine grandchildren, and one great granddaughter.

CONTACT THE AUTHOR

https://patriciadaboh.com

patriciadaboh9@gmail.com

Made in the USA
Columbia, SC
15 February 2019